HOW CAN I HELP?

Rory
the
garden bird

Frances Rodgers and **Ben Grisdale**

Written and illustrated by
Frances Rodgers and Ben Grisdale

Editor Abi Luscombe
Project Art Editor Charlotte Bull
Managing Editor Laura Gilbert
Publishing Manager Francesca Young
Publishing Coordinator Issy Walsh
Production Editor Dragana Puvacic
Production Controller Isabell Schart
Deputy Art Director Mabel Chan
Publishing Director Sarah Larter

First published in Great Britain in 2021
by Dorling Kindersley Limited
DK, One Embassy Gardens,
8 Viaduct Gardens, London, SW11 7BW

The authorised representative in the EEA is
Dorling Kindersley Verlag GmbH. Arnulfstr.
124, 80636 Munich, Germany

For the curious
www.dk.com

**The item should be returned or renewed
by the last date stamped below.**

Dylid dychwelyd neu adnewyddu'r eitem erbyn
y dyddiad olaf sydd wedi'i stampio isod.

PILLGWENLLY

To renew visit / Adnewyddwch ar
www.newport.gov.uk/libraries

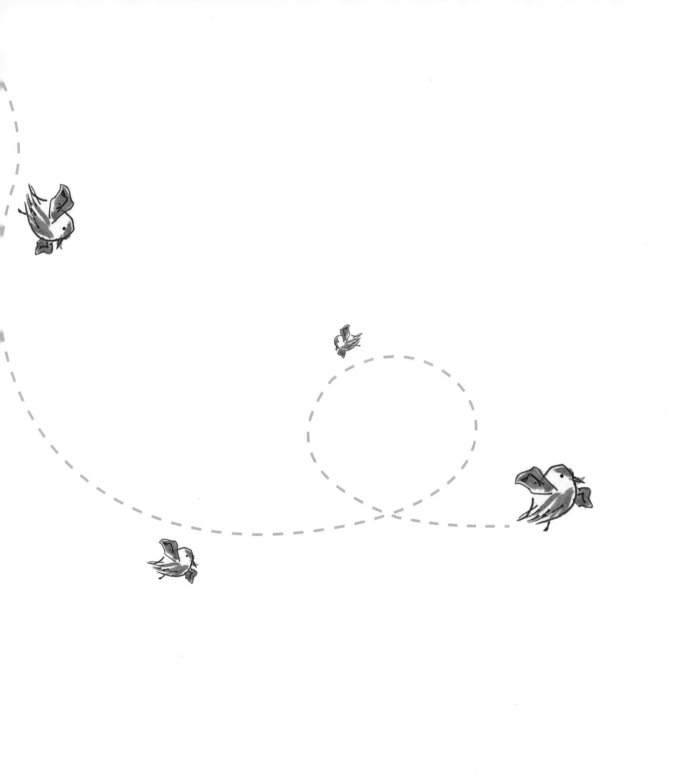

Hello, my name is Rory.
I am a garden bird and
I need your help.

**Let me visit your garden
for food and water.**

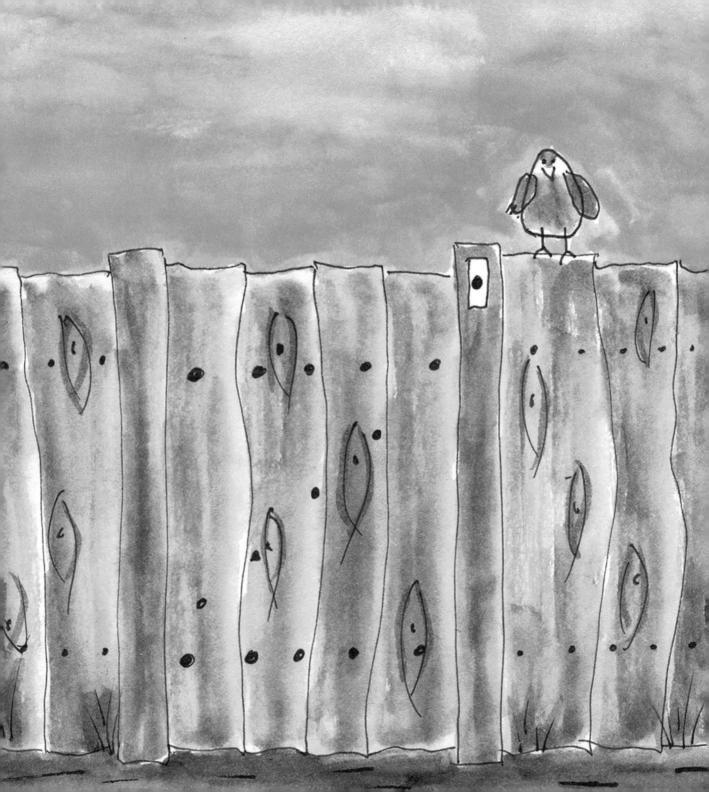

I like to drink and
wash in water.

Please give me a bird bath.

I like to eat bird seed
in the summer.

I like to eat balls of
food in the winter.

I also like to eat bugs
and flies, so please plant
flowers to attract them.

**Trees are good for food
and I feel safe in them**.

**Please give me a home
in your trees**.

Rubbish in your garden can be a danger to me.

Please keep your garden tidy.

Please do not use nets in your garden.

I can get stuck in them.

Please keep your bird feeders and bath clean to stop me getting poorly.

Thank you for all your help.

Why do we need to protect house sparrows?

Rory is a type of bird called a house sparrow. House sparrows live in busy places like towns and cities, in nests, bushes, holes, and even in gaps in buildings.

Unfortunately, these sparrows are endangered, which means that, one day, we may not see them any more.

It is not just house sparrows that are at risk, but other types of sparrows are also in trouble. That is why we all need to do what we can to help these little animals!

Where in the world?

House sparrows were first found in Europe and parts of Asia and northern Africa, but they have since been introduced to other parts of the world. These feathered friends can now be found on every continent except Antarctica!

Streaky brown, black, and grey feathers on its back →

Male sparrow

Grey patc on its hea ↖

A house sparrow can be up to 15 cm (6 in) from beak to tail – that is roughly the same length as a bank note!

Light brown or grey colouring on its tummy ←

Garden birds around the world

There are lots of different garden birds in the world, as well as the house sparrow. Here are just a few that can be found...

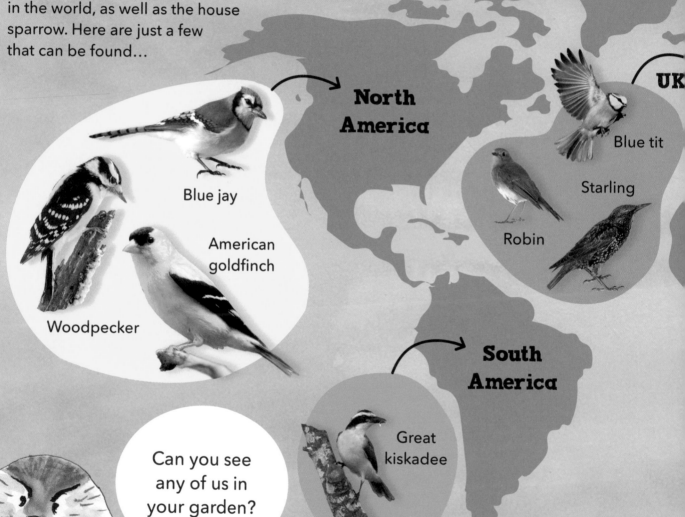

North America

Blue jay

American goldfinch

Woodpecker

UK

Blue tit

Starling

Robin

South America

Great kiskadee

Can you see any of us in your garden?

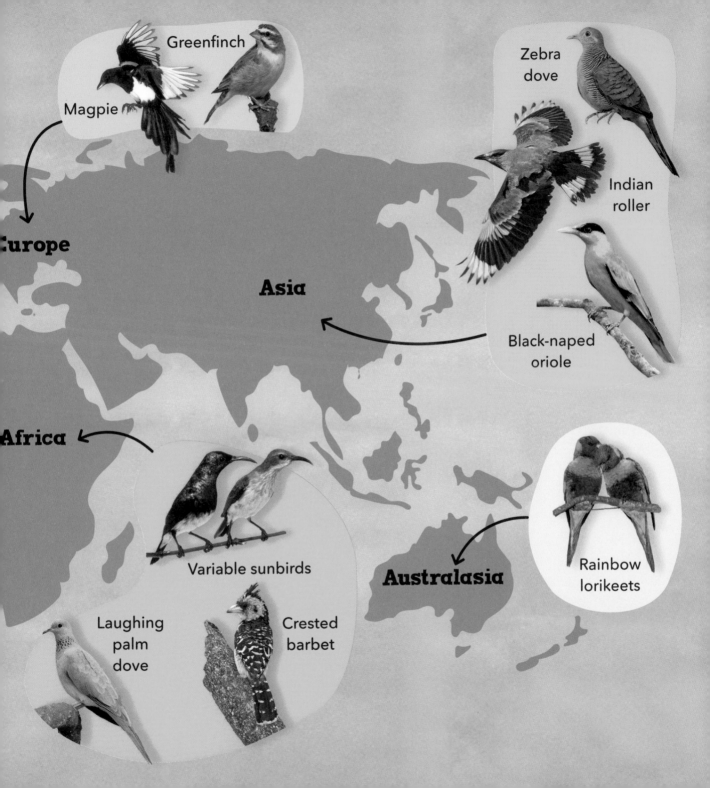

Greenfinch

Magpie

Europe

Zebra dove

Indian roller

Asia

Black-naped oriole

Africa

Variable sunbirds

Laughing palm dove

Crested barbet

Australasia

Rainbow lorikeets

Acknowledgements

The publisher would like to thank the following for their kind permission to reproduce their photographs:

(Key: a-above; b-below/bottom; c-center; f-far; l-left; r-right; t-top)

34 Getty Images: James Warwick (tr, cl/x2, cr). **35 Chris Gomersall Photography:** (cra). **Dreamstime.com:** Victortyakht (tl); Wildlife World (clb). **36 Getty Images / iStock:** Dgwildlife (c). **37 Dreamstime.com:** Isselee (c). **38 Dorling Kindersley:** Alan Murphy (bc). **Dreamstime.com:** Steve Byland (cl); Svetlana Foote (ca); Tony Northrup / Acanonguy (cb); Vasyl Helevachuk (cr). **Getty Images:** Stockbyte / John Foxx (cra). **39 Dreamstime.com:** Peter Betts (bc); PeterWaters (crb); Davemontreuil (bl). **Getty Images / iStock:** PrinPrince (cr)

All other images © Dorling Kindersley
For further information see: www.dkimages.com

About the author and illustrator

Ben and Frances are husband and wife and they live in Newcastle upon Tyne, Engla
They are passionate about helping the wild
in their garden. In the middle of a summer
night, Frances woke with an idea to create
books to encourage young children
to do the same.

Frances wrote the books and Ben
illustrated them and they brought to life
Roly the hedgehog, *Rory the garden bird*,
Rosy the bumblebee, and *Roxy the butterfl*